ETHICS
AT
WORK

THEOLOGY OF WORK ＞ PROJECT

ETHICS
AT
WORK

THE BIBLE AND YOUR WORK
Study Series

HENDRICKSON
PUBLISHERS

Theology of Work
The Bible and Your Work Study Series: Ethics at Work

© 2017 by Hendrickson Publishers Marketing, LLC
P.O. Box 3473
Peabody, Massachusetts 01961-3473
www.hendrickson.com

ISBN 978-1-61970-892-1

William Messenger, Executive Editor, Theology of Work Project
Sean McDonough, Biblical Editor, Theology of Work Project
Patricia Anders, Editorial Director, Hendrickson Publishers

Contributors:

Christopher Gilbert, "Ethics at Work" Bible Study
Alistair Mackenzie and Wayne Kirkland, "Ethics at Work," Theology of Work Project article

The Theology of Work Project is an independent, international organization dedicated to researching, writing, and distributing materials with a biblical perspective on work. The Project's primary mission is to produce resources covering every book of the Bible plus major topics in today's workplaces. Wherever possible, the Project collaborates with other faith-and-work organizations, churches, universities and seminaries to help equip people for meaningful, productive work of every kind.

Printed in the United States of America

First Printing—April 2017

Contents

The Theology of Work

Work is not only a human calling, but also a divine one. "In the beginning God created the heavens and the earth." God worked to create us and created us to work. "The LORD God took the man and put him in the garden of Eden to till it and keep it" (Gen. 2:15). God also created work to be good, even if it's hard to see in a fallen world. To this day, God calls us to work to support ourselves and to serve others (Eph. 4:28).

Work can accomplish many of God's purposes for our lives—the basic necessities of food and shelter, as well as a sense of fulfillment and joy. Our work can create ways to help people thrive; it can discover the depths of God's creation; and it can bring us into wonderful relationships with co-workers and those who benefit from our work (customers, clients, patients, and so forth).

Yet many people face drudgery, boredom, or exploitation at work. We have bad bosses, hostile relationships, and unfriendly work environments. Our work seems useless, unappreciated, faulty, frustrating. We don't get paid enough. We get stuck in dead-end jobs or laid off or fired. We fail. Our skills become obsolete. It's a struggle just to make ends meet. But how can this be if God created work to be good—and what can we do about it? God's answers for these questions must be somewhere in the Bible, but where?

The Theology of Work Project's mission has been to study what the Bible says about work and to develop resources to apply the

Christian faith to our work. It turns out that every book of the Bible gives practical, relevant guidance that can help us do our jobs better, improve our relationships at work, support ourselves, serve others more effectively, and find meaning and value in our work. The Bible shows us how to live all of life—including work—in Christ. Only in Jesus can we and our work be transformed to become the blessing it was always meant to be.

To put it another way, if we are not following Christ during the 100,000 hours of our lives that we spend at work, are we really following Christ? Our lives are more than just one day a week at church. The fact is that God cares about our life *every day of the week*. But how do we become equipped to follow Jesus at work? In the same ways we become equipped for every aspect of life in Christ—listening to sermons, modeling our lives on others' examples, praying for God's guidance, and most of all by studying the Bible and putting it into practice.

This Theology of Work series contains a variety of books to help you apply the Scriptures and Christian faith to your work. This Bible study is one volume in the series The Bible and Your Work. It is intended for those who want to explore what the Bible says about work and how to apply it to their work in positive, practical ways. Although it can be used for individual study, Bible study is especially effective with a group of people committed to practicing what they read in Scripture. In this way, we gain from one another's perspectives and are encouraged to actually *do* what we read in Scripture. Because of the direct focus on work, The Bible and Your Work studies are especially suited for Bible studies *at* work or *with* other people in similar occupations. The following lessons are designed for thirty-minute lunch breaks (or perhaps breakfast before work) during a five-day work week.

Christians today recognize God's calling to us in and through our work—for ourselves and for those whom we serve. May God use this book to help you follow Christ in every sphere of life and work.

Will Messenger, Executive Editor
Theology of Work Project

Introduction

Throughout the Theology of Work Bible study series, we demonstrate that for Christians work finds its meaning from who God is and what God does. God is at work in the world, and we are workers made in the image of God to partner with God in his continuing work. Therefore, we take a responsible view of the world, our place and work in it, and the values we take to our places of employment. For this reason, we look to cultivate a deeper understanding of ethics in the workplace.

 Food for Thought

What do you think of when someone says, "She's a very ethical person"? What words would you use to explain your sense of "ethics"? (It will be interesting to see how this compares to the conclusions you come to by the end of this study!)

_____

_____

_____

_____

_____

_____

The words *ethics* and *ethical* are used often but frequently misunderstood. In popular culture, *ethics* can be narrowly construed: "He has a great work ethic" often means he's a hard worker. Or it may be used as a euphemism for someone who's a workaholic.

At best, *ethical* means someone who operates by a system of values. In the workplace this is often associated with the idea of "being professional," or more simply, being honest and upright in dealings with others. An ethical person wouldn't try to mistreat, defraud, or take advantage of another. These words are often used about an individual in contrast to a pervading stereotype of businesspeople. Some leaders or companies have tarnished the image of business by prioritizing profits over people, or by promoting aggressive selling techniques that are considered predatory, especially on the less educated, the naive, and the elderly.

For some Christians, *ethics* might sound suspiciously like a code of conduct, a form of legalism leading to works righteousness instead of work done from faith in Jesus. But in Christian life, *ethics* is about knowing and doing what is good or right, and workplace ethics is about knowing and doing what is good or right at work.

Often, agreement on ethical principles might be hard to reach. It can seem as if people do what is right in their own eyes and then regard their behavior as "ethical" because they chose it. But Christians find their guidance primarily from the biblical narrative, in the context of their community of faith in Christ, where through prayer and the Spirit of God they make sense of their circumstances to determine the best possible response. We can apply these same resources to help us decide what is ethical or moral at work. (In this study, *ethics* and *morality* will be used to mean the same thing.)

Using three "C's," we will look at three common approaches to ethics that have guided the morality of Christians and also the world at large:

1. *Command*—What do the rules say is the right way to act?

2. *Consequences*—What actions are most likely to bring about the best outcome?

3. *Character*—What kind of moral person do I want to be or become?

Christian ethics are distinguished by the values they incorporate, derived from the various genres that comprise the sixty-six books of the Bible. There are biblical commands (also called principles), biblically desired outcomes, and biblical character traits (also called virtues). These commands, outcomes, and virtues form the basis of a Christian's decisions, actions, and moral development.

In developing a Christian ethic, we will explore how the Bible illustrates each of these three approaches. Then we'll consider whether combining these three in some way gives us a more balanced and integrated approach to ethics. Finally, we'll consider how to live with the reality that our world is broken and far from the way we know it ought to be. This means that for any given situation there may not be a perfect ethical cure. We must learn to choose, like with prescription medicine, the best of approximate options.

 Food for Thought

Notice the use of the word *custom* in Acts 25:16: "I told them that it was not the *custom* of the Romans to hand over anyone before the accused had met the accusers face to face and had been given an opportunity to make a defense against the charge." How does this word function in the passage? In 1 Corinthians 15:33, this word is translated as "morals" or "character": "Do not be deceived:

'Bad *company* ruins good *morals*'" (italics added). What do these verses tell you about the use of the word *ethos* (which has two meanings in common Greek usage—habit or custom, and ordinance or law—and from which derives the word *ethics*)?

_____

_____

_____

_____

_____

_____

_____

In light of the definition above, how do we define *ethics* today? In *Choosing the Good: Christian Ethics in a Complex World*, Dennis Hollinger says that ethics is "the systematic study of standards of right and wrong, justice and injustice, virtue and vice, with a view to applying those standards in the realities of our lives." Stanley J. Grenz, author of *The Moral Quest*, suggests that Christian ethical living is concerned with "ordering our steps in every situation of life according to the fundamental faith commitments we share as Christians." And still a third definition, put forth by Alistair Mackenzie and Wayne Kirkland in *Just Decisions*, states: "Christian ethics is the attempt to provide a framework and method for making decisions, that seeks to honor God as revealed in Scripture, follow the example of Jesus and be responsive to the Spirit, to achieve outcomes that further God's purposes in the world."

In chapters 1 and 2 of this study, we will lay out three approaches to ethics as illustrated in the Bible. Then from chapter 3 onward, we will develop a Christian approach to ethics as applied to work through a case study of a real workplace situation. The goal is that when you are finished with this study, you will have developed practical Christian ethical principles you can apply to the various work circumstances you face.

Food for Thought

What ethical dilemmas do you face in your work today? What principles have you applied to them in the past?

_____

_____

_____

_____

_____

_____

_____

Prayer

Pause for a few moments of silence to reflect on this lesson. Then offer a prayer, either spontaneous or by using the following:

Lord,

So often I make decisions on automatic pilot, without deliberate forethought about ethical considerations. In this study, help me to leave aside my preconceived notions and construct a more thoughtful, deliberate ethical structure for my decision-making. I want to reflect your heart in my work.

Amen.

Chapter 1

The First C—"Command"

Lesson #1: An Overview

A generally agreed upon basis for ethics can be described simply as command, consequence, and character.

Command

The command approach asks, "According to the rules, is this action right or wrong in itself?" It proposes that actions are inherently right or wrong, as defined by a set of rules or duties, whether given by divine command, tradition, natural law, rational logic, or another source. Christian ethics looks to commands given by God or derived from God's character revealed in the Bible.

 Food for Thought

Consider Jeremiah 29:7: "But seek the welfare of the city where I have sent you into exile, and pray to the Lord on its behalf, for in its welfare you will find your welfare." How does this apply to your work as a specific command?

_____

_____

_____

_____

_____

_____

_____

_____

Consequence

The consequence approach asks, "Will this action produce good or bad results?" It is often called the teleological approach, because it argues that end results determine the morally correct course of action. In the consequence approach, the most moral course of action may be decided by asking the following questions:

1. What will result in the greatest good? Utilitarianism, for example, defines the greatest good as whatever will bring the greatest happiness to the greatest number of people.

2. What best advances one's self-interest? Ethical egoism proposes that what is in the best interest of all people is for each person to pursue their own best interest, within certain limits.

3. What will produce the ends most in accord with God's intent for his creation? This approach can focus on subordinate goals (such as gaining better quality of life for a disabled person) or an ultimate goal (such as glorifying God and enjoying him forever). In the case of complicated circumstances, this approach tries to calculate which actions will maximize the balance of good over evil.

 *Food for Thought*

Consider whether utilitarianism or ethical egoism have a place in Christian forms of ethics. In 2 Kings 20:16–19, King Hezekiah acts out of self-interest:

> Then Isaiah said to Hezekiah, "Hear the word of the LORD: Days are coming when all that is in your house, and that which your ancestors have stored up until this day, shall be carried to Babylon; nothing shall be left, says the LORD. Some of your own sons who are born to you shall be taken away; they shall be eunuchs in the palace of the king of Babylon." Then Hezekiah said to Isaiah, "The word of the LORD that you have spoken is good." For he thought, "Why not, if there will be peace and security in my days?"

Does this Bible passage paint a utilitarianism or ethical egoism view of consequences, and how does it do so?

_____

_____

_____

_____

_____

_____

_____

_____

Character

The character approach asks, "Is the actor a good person with good motives?" Whether an action is moral is therefore decided by questions about character, motives, and the community that shapes these attitudes. This is often called "virtue ethics." Since the beginning of the Christian era, virtues have been recognized as an essential element of Christian ethics. However, from the time of the sixteenth-century Reformation until the late twentieth century, virtue ethics and consequential ethics were overshadowed by command ethics in most Protestant thinking.

 Food for Thought

Nehemiah 1–2 describes what Nehemiah does when he learns about the danger and disgrace facing the Jews in Jerusalem. First he weeps, fasts, and prays. Then he asks his boss for help sourcing materials to rebuild Jerusalem's wall. Finally, he galvanizes the Jewish people to join in the rebuilding work together. What character traits seem to drive Nehemiah on his mission to rebuild and restore the community of God in Jerusalem?

_____

_____

_____

_____

_____

_____

_____

_____

Prayer

Pause for a few moments of silence to reflect on this lesson. Then offer a prayer, either spontaneous or by using the following:

Lord,

Help me to discern your ethical concerns in all that I undertake. As I read Scripture, help me to see where command, consequence, or character—or a mix of these—applies to my daily circumstances.

Amen.

Lesson #2: Command—A Biblical Rule for Every Situation?

Many biblical verses provide grounding principles that apply to our work. From the first chapters of Genesis, God models a seven-day pattern of work and rest that God's people are called to emulate (Gen. 2:2; Exod. 20:9–11). The Psalms also commend a daily rhythm of work and rest (Ps. 104:19–23), and they extol the virtues of honest work as well (Ps. 128:2). In his two letters to the Thessalonians, Paul praises hard work over idleness (1 Thess. 2:9; 2 Thess. 3:7–10). The book of Proverbs contains similar exhortations to work diligently (Prov. 6:6). Manual work is not to be despised: even a king works with his hands (1 Sam. 11:5), the prophets denounce the idle rich (Amos 6:3–6), and Jesus himself worked as an artisan (Mark 6:3). And this is just a quick skim of the commands in Scripture relating to work.

The Businessman's Topical Bible and *The Businesswoman's Topical Bible* identify one hundred common workplace problems, using 1,550 Bible verses to point to answers. But no set of commands can be vast enough to cover all the issues that arise in our modern workplaces. Many of the ethical questions we face have no precedent in biblical times. Is it ethical to award stock options based on performance? Is it ethical to advertise a product to entice people to buy more of it? Is it ethical to have hiring preferences for underrepresented ethnic groups? None of these situations are directly addressed by a biblical command.

Scripture does, however, offer clarity on many issues. There are injunctions against certain actions—stealing, lying, and coveting among them. There are also positive commands—to love our enemies, act justly, and care for the poor, just to name a few. But out of this, it is impossible to develop a comprehensive scriptural code that applies to every situation we encounter. The Pharisees tried to do so in their time, only for Jesus to castigate them for straining out gnats and swallowing camels!

So while the Bible can't be turned into a comprehensive rule book for ethics in the modern marketplace, it does contain some important rules we can use to inform our actions in the ethical dilemmas we face.

 Food for Thought

What are some Bible verses that have helped you in your work life? Can you think of biblical commands that would never fit in your workplace? In what ways does your reading of Scripture affect the way you do your job today?

_____

_____

_____

_____

_____

_____

Can We Find Simplified Guiding Principles from the Biblical Commands?

The most common attempts to distill the essence of biblical commands emphasize the importance of the Ten Commandments (Exod. 20:1–17; Deut. 5:4–21), the Beatitudes (Matt. 5:3–11), or quotes from the book of Proverbs. For example, Larry Burkett, in his *Business by the Book: The Complete Guide of Biblical Principles for Business Men and Women,* lays out "Six Basic Biblical Business Minimums":

1. Reflect Christ in your business practices

2. Be accountable

3. Provide a quality product at a fair price

4. Honor your creditors

5. Treat your employees fairly

6. Treat your customers fairly

Many such lists have been published. While they address a felt need to be told exactly how to act in modern business, they take away our focus from the Bible and the insight that comes from struggling with the word of God.

A more biblical approach comes from *Business through the Eyes of Faith* by Richard C. Chewning. This book takes the command to love our neighbor as its primary source material, using Micah 6:8 as the organizing principle for determining how God would have us apply love in business:

> He has told you, O mortal, what is good; and what does the Lord require of you but to do justice, and to love kindness and to walk humbly with your God?

Here, love as applied through justice, kindness, and faithfulness becomes the foundational principal of an ethical framework. Jesus also emphasizes the importance of these same three elements in Matthew 23:23:

> "Woe to you, scribes and Pharisees, hypocrites! For you tithe mint, dill, and cumin, and have neglected the weightier matters of the law: justice and mercy and faith. It is these you ought to have practiced without neglecting the others."

This direct engagement with Scripture seems closer to the heart of Christian ethics.

 Food for Thought

How do you feel about the "Six Basic Biblical Business Minimums" that Burkett puts forth? Do they reflect your own business principles or your understanding of Scripture? What about the text from Micah 6:8? Does that feel like enough of a guiding principle to help you make business decisions?

_____

_____

_____

_____

_____

_____

_____

Prayer

Pause for a few moments of silence to reflect on this lesson. Then offer a prayer, either spontaneous or by using the following:

> Lord,
>
> *Your word is as vast and rich as you are. Help me read with an eye to see your wisdom revealed. I look to you for lessons to guide my work and for the strength to uphold your commands.*
>
> *Amen.*

Lesson #3: Is There Just One Clear Command?

We might wonder whether there is one biblical command upon which all the others are built. John Maxwell's book *There's No Such Thing as "Business" Ethics* identifies the Golden Rule as the summation of all other biblical directives: "Do to others as you would have them do to you; for this is the law and the prophets" (Matt. 7:12). In practical application, this involves asking a single question: "How would I like to be treated in this situation?" Maxwell expands the Golden Rule into several principles he believes apply to most business situations:

- Treat people better than they treat you

- Walk the second mile

- Help people who can't help you

- Do right when it's natural to do wrong

- Keep your promises even when it hurts

Perhaps these are all best practices for a Christian in business. However, transforming the Golden Rule into a pithy list complicates a fundamental biblical commandment with interpolations of its meaning, a very subjective exercise.

In his book *Situation Ethics*, Joseph Fletcher chooses a different single commandment to apply to all questions of ethics: "You shall love your neighbor as yourself" (Matt. 22:39). But the problem remains the same: How do we determine the most loving action? While Maxwell doesn't transmute the Golden Rule into a list of imperatives, his approach does demonstrate the drawbacks of elevating one principle over all others. Doing so can lead us to deceive ourselves regarding the complexities of the ethical dilemmas we face.

 Food for Thought

Consider a situation you have faced at work and how it might have been resolved by applying the Golden Rule. What other maxims does this make you think of? Are they different from Maxwell's list?

_____

_____

_____

_____

_____

_____

_____

Three Balancing Principles

Alexander Hill, president of InterVarsity Christian Fellowship/ USA, sees the character of God as the source of biblical commands or principles. While Hill starts with God's character of holiness, justice, and love, his method is not considered a form of character-based ethics (as discussed in the next chapter), because when it comes to determining appropriate behavior, Hill's method is to develop rules and principles. He says the laws we set—our rules and practices—should bring about holiness, justice, and love.

Hill says that Christian ethics requires all three principles to be taken into account all the time. Each, like the leg of a three-legged stool, balances the other two. Overemphasizing the importance of one at the expense of the others always leads to a distortion in ethical thinking.

For example, an overemphasis on holiness can easily lead to rules that require Christians to withdraw from the world. A bias for justice can produce oppressive penalties for breaking societal rules. And favoring love can lead to fuzzy boundaries and lack of accountability.

Hill's approach would seem to provide for a better balance than relying on a single principle. It also provides some help for exploring both personal and social ethical dilemmas. However, God's character traits of love, justice, and holiness still need explaining by reference to his other biblical actions.

Prayer

Pause for a few moments of silence to reflect on this lesson. Then offer a prayer, either spontaneous or by using the following:

Lord,

As I go about my work today, help me see where I can embody your holiness. Help me pursue justice in my workplace. And help me balance these ideals with love for those around me.

Amen.

Chapter 2

The Second and Third C's— "Consequences" and "Character"

Lesson #1: Consequences and Character

Consequences

The fundamental question for the consequences approach to ethics is, "Will it produce good results?" or "Which choice will produce the best result?" The most moral course of action is therefore determined by its likely outcome. A consequences approach to ethics involves anticipating and calculating the results of different courses of action, and then choosing the best possible result.

Because so many people think of the Bible as a rule book, it is perhaps surprising to discover how often the Scriptures encourage readers to consider the consequences of their actions and let this influence their decision-making.

Proverbs is full of warnings and promises—pithy sayings that spell out the likely outcomes of certain actions. For example, Proverbs 14:14 states, "The perverse get what their ways deserve, and the good, what their deeds deserve."

Food for Thought

Can you recall a moment at work when you decided on a course
of action based on the potential consequences? Did you get what
your deeds deserved, as Proverbs 14:14 suggests?

_____

_____

_____

_____

_____

_____

_____

_____

Jesus warns his listeners to weigh carefully the consequences of
their decisions: "You will know them by their fruits" (Matt. 7:16).
In fact, in one sense Jesus' whole life and ministry can be viewed
as a living example of making decisions for the greater good.

Jesus' Beatitudes also display an implicit understanding of cause
and effect. If you want to be "filled," then hunger and thirst after
righteousness (Matt 5:6). The rest of the Sermon on the Mount
also demonstrates this link between actions and consequences,
such as in the following passages:

> "Let your light shine before others, so that they may see your good
> works and give glory to your Father in heaven." (Matt. 5:16)

> "Come to terms quickly with your accuser while you are on the way
> to court with him, or your accuser may hand you over to the judge,
> and the judge to the guard, and you will be thrown into prison."
> (Matt. 5:25)

"But when you give alms, do not let your left hand know what your
right hand is doing, so that your alms may be done in secret; and
your Father who sees in secret will reward you." (Matt. 6:3–4)

Considering the consequences is an important biblical approach
to ethical decision-making. Unfortunately, determining whether
a particular consequence is good is not always as straightforward
as it might seem. We must wrestle with questions such as:

- "What is good?"

- "Good for whom?"

- "Does a good end always justify the means?"

- "Does the context influence what is good?"

This is one reason why it is important to consider other ethical
frameworks alongside consequences.

 Food for Thought

In the workplace, we often have to decide what the greater good is,
especially when budget or staffing is involved. How have you applied ethics to these decisions in the past? How will you apply these
Bible verses on cause and effect to your decisions in the future?

_____

_____

_____

_____

_____

_____

Character

With the virtue, or character, approach to ethics we ask, "What type of person should I become?" We presuppose that if a person develops good character, then he or she is more likely to do the right thing. Virtue ethics is therefore more about becoming a good person than about determining what is good in the heat of the moment.

Virtue ethics also recognizes that knowing the right thing to do doesn't always ensure you will actually do it. Doing the right thing takes strength of character. Virtue ethics aims to develop the habit of doing the right thing alongside knowing what the right thing to do is. It is concerned with allowing the character of God to shape our own characters. Are we becoming loving, just, merciful, and holy in character? These need to be virtues that are ingrained in us as default settings, as in Ephesians 5:1, "Therefore be imitators of God, as beloved children."

There are several reasons why this is important. First of all, we don't always have the time and ability to reason our way through complex issues. Most of our decisions are made instantaneously, on the fly. We have only seconds to decide how to relate to a co-worker, sort out a problem, advise a customer, or motivate an underperforming individual. Developing good character allows us to more quickly perceive how to act ethically, compared to having to reason every situation from scratch.

Second, our character automatically shapes much of what we decide. Even when we think we are doing ethical reasoning, we are often simply following our established character, rationalizing our actions in the process. Because of this, our ethical decisions are largely determined by who we are (the type of character and values we've embodied) rather than our decision-making process.

Third, we are not always individuals freely making personal deci-sions. Our actions are largely shaped by our communities. Char-acter and community are intertwined with our values in ways that are inseparable when it comes to talking about ethics. As we develop good character, we are simultaneously improving the character of the communities we belong to. This will make it more possible to act ethically in the future.

Theologian David Cook argues that we rarely make conscious moral decisions anyway. Whether we know it or not, almost all of our ethics *is* character ethics. Most of the time, we don't think about the moral dilemma; we simply respond to it. If this is the case and our reactions are substantially instinctive, then devel-oping godly character is even more important. If we make many of our ethical choices automatically, then godly people have a greater chance of making good choices.

 Food for Thought

Can you describe a time in your work when you were either pos-itively or negatively affected by decisions someone made "on the fly"? How did the character of the decision-maker influence his or her decision?

_____

_____

_____

_____

_____

_____

Prayer

Pause for a few moments of silence to reflect on this lesson. Then offer a prayer, either spontaneous or by using the following:

Lord,

I want to develop a godly character and know how to respond to situations as you would have me do. Spirit of God, please guide me into knowing the mind of Christ, so that I may become ever more like him.

Amen.

Lesson #2: But Which Virtues?

Just as the command and consequence approaches to ethics have to determine which commands and consequences are truly good, so the character approach must determine which virtues are desirable. Aristotle emphasized the classical Greek virtues of justice, fortitude, prudence, and temperance. Saint Ambrose agreed that these were implicit in the Bible, but he also added faith and hope, as in 1 Corinthians 13:13: "So now faith, hope, and love abide, these three; but the greatest of these is love" (ESV). Thomas Aquinas contrasted a list of virtues with examples of their opposites: pride, greed, lust, malicious envy, gluttony, wrath, and sloth—what he called the seven deadly vices.

With each theological innovation, however, the problem still remains: Are the core virtues adequately listed? And if not, from where should they be derived?

 *Food for Thought*

Do you think these lists of virtues and vices cover everything you
value in your own character? Would you add anything? If so, what?

_____

_____

_____

_____

_____

_____

_____

_____

For colleagues Glen Stassen and David P. Gushee in their book
Kingdom Ethics: Following Jesus in Contemporary Context,
the starting place for Christians in the quest for guiding virtues is Jesus' Sermon on the Mount, especially the Beatitudes
(Matt. 5:3–9 ESV):

> "Blessed are the poor in spirit, for theirs is the kingdom of heaven.
>
> Blessed are those who mourn, for they shall be comforted.
>
> Blessed are the meek, for they shall inherit the earth.
>
> Blessed are those who hunger and thirst for righteousness, for
> they shall be satisfied.
>
> Blessed are the merciful, for they shall receive mercy.
>
> Blessed are the pure in heart, for they shall see God.
>
> Blessed are the peacemakers, for they shall be called sons of God"

Poverty of spirit, mercy, the thirst/hunger for justice, meekness/ humility, peacemaking, and compassion—these are some of the key qualities we should nurture.

 Food for Thought

How do you cultivate the virtues listed in the Beatitudes in your own life? Do some virtues come more easily to you than others?

_____

_____

_____

_____

_____

_____

_____

_____

In his letter to the Philippians, Paul writes,

> Do nothing from selfish ambition or conceit, but in humility count others more significant than yourselves. Let each of you look not only to his own interests, but also to the interests of others. Have this mind among yourselves, which is yours in Christ Jesus.
>
> (Phil. 2:3–5 ESV)

Paul concurs with the Christian theologians listed above that Jesus should be our model and that we are called to imitate his example.

Prayer

Pause for a few moments of silence to reflect on this lesson. Then offer a prayer, either spontaneous or by using the following:

Lord,

I often long for rules because they are easier than working on my character. Please help me grow more like you and trust your Spirit in maturing me into the character of Jesus. Make me hungry and thirsty for this work of your Spirit in my life.

Amen.

Lesson #3: But Which Jesus?

The New Testament writings exhort Christians to conform to the image of Jesus, as in 1 John 3:2 (ESV): "Beloved, we are God's children now, and what we will be has not yet appeared; but we know that when he appears we shall be like him, because we shall see him as he is." Unfortunately, research in the United States suggests that few Christians take this to heart. Robin Gill, in his book *Churchgoing and Christian Ethics*, found that the only distinctive ethical differences between churchgoers and secular society regard a few issues of sexual conduct, personal honesty, and the accumulation of wealth. In most other respects, we are shaped more by the values of our culture than by the ethics of Jesus.

In wealthy Western communities, socioeconomic, political, and environmental implications of Jesus' life and teachings are too easily filtered out, leaving us with a Jesus who addresses only a small range of "personal" moral issues. There is a gravitational pull on all Christians to remake Jesus in our own image. We easily reframe Jesus' commands, pointers to consequences, and character in order to remove his challenges to our inherited way of life.

 *Food for Thought*

Do you interact with people of diverse ethnicities at church? Has this challenged you to reflect on your own cultural givens? If not, are you aware of any ways your cultural milieu shapes your understanding of the gospel?

_____

_____

_____

_____

_____

_____

_____

_____

In his book *In Praise of Virtue*, Benjamin Farley writes:

> The New Testament, in concert with the Hebrew Bible, emphasizes the indispensable context of the believing community. . . . It is within this nurturing context of faith, hope and love . . . that the Christian life, as a process, unfolds. It is never a matter of the individual alone, pitted against an alien and hostile culture, that constitutes the epicenter of Christian moral action.

Unfortunately, most churches fail to address workplace and business ethical issues.

The founder of Enron, Kenneth Lay, was regarded as a devout Christian by his church community. Nevertheless, in 2006 he was convicted on six counts of conspiracy and ten counts of securities fraud. Bernie Ebbers of WorldCom, also highly regarded by his church, was convicted on nine counts of conspiracy, securities fraud, and false regulatory filings amounting to $11 billion. When such ethical blindness is exhibited by "devout Christians," there is urgent need for Christian education in marketplace ethics.

A community that seeks to retell, understand, and live out the gospel story in the workplace will be more likely to produce whistle-blowers rather than exponents of fraud. Such communities seek a clearer picture of the character of Jesus, and allow him to ask hard and uncomfortable questions that confront their own limited view of virtue.

 Food for Thought

Is there a blind spot in your church when it comes to teaching ethics in your workplace? If so, how would you suggest your church plug that gap?

_____

_____

_____

_____

_____

_____

Summary

We have seen that command, consequence, and character are three different approaches to understanding ethics. In actual ethical dilemmas, however, we discover that some combination of these approaches is necessary for resolution. We are unlikely to apply a specific command or rule without also considering the consequence for all concerned. At the same time, we will choose between different anticipated consequences according to how we prioritize different commands. Whatever our decision, it is character that finally dictates how we follow through.

In the coming chapters, we will apply these ethical frameworks to case studies in decision-making. In doing so, we will see the interplay of these three approaches and understand how they affect our decision-making.

Prayer

Pause for a few moments of silence to reflect on this lesson. Then offer a prayer, either spontaneous or by using the following:

Lord,

As I face the decisions before me today, help me hear the voice of Jesus in the Gospels. Give me a desire to obey your commands. Show me your empathy for consequences. And grow my character through your grace.

Amen.

Chapter 3

Case Study—The Broken Gearbox

Lesson #1: The Problem and the First Issues of the "Command" Approach

Wayne Kirkland is a Theology of Work contributor and coauthor of the book *Where's God on Monday?* He also sells cars for a living. He once sold a secondhand Toyota Camry to a customer in good faith, which had been checked thoroughly before the sale and was found in above-average condition for its price range.

Twelve months later, the customer calls Wayne about a recent problem with the automatic transmission. He asks Wayne what he will do to fix it. Despite the time lapse since the sale, Wayne is sympathetic to the client's plight. He wonders, "Should I take responsibility for the problem and carry the cost of fixing the gearbox?"

This would mean choosing to accept a financial loss on the Camry, as the added cost of repair for Wayne will exceed the value of the car's sale price. Wayne asks the customer to wait a day while he considers the issue carefully. After the phone call, Wayne finds many concerns crossing his mind:

- How will his faith in Christ influence his decision?

- What commands should a Christian obey?

- What consequences should a Christian seek?

- What does Christian character call for?

We will follow Wayne's journey as he considers his best approach.

 Food for Thought

What is your initial response to Wayne's dilemma? Note carefully toward which approach you tend to gravitate: command, consequence, or character. Why is that particular approach attractive to you?

_____

_____

_____

_____

_____

_____

_____

_____

Command: A Legal Responsibility

Wayne's first impulse is to consider whether there is a simple rule or command that could help him decide the right thing to do. First, he wonders about his legal responsibility. Wayne knows that the Consumer Guarantees Act in New Zealand (where he's based) mandates that a vehicle be of acceptable quality. Specifically, the vehicle must be:

1. Fit for the purpose that type of vehicle is normally used

2. Acceptable in finish and appearance

3. Free from minor defects

4. Safe

5. Durable (in other words, the vehicle is able to be used for its normal purposes for a reasonable time after purchase)

6. The age and price of a vehicle must be taken into account when deciding whether it meets an acceptable quality

 Food for Thought

Looking at the requirements of the law here, what is likely to be the main legal issue that has to be satisfied? What do you think Wayne will be required to do?

_____

_____

_____

_____

_____

_____

_____

There is no clearly defined answer to what is "a reasonable time" for durability, so Wayne's legal obligations are sketchy. For a seven-year-old Camry with medium mileage, three months or

5,000 kilometers (about 3,100 miles) would be considered a "reasonable" period for Wayne to be legally obliged to repair the car. But a customer might well think that six or twelve months was "a reasonable time," although that would unlikely be upheld if it were ever tested in a court of law.

Wayne asks the customer how many kilometers he has driven the car over the past twelve months. The answer is 22,000 kilometers (about 13,600 miles). This suggests to Wayne that he has no legal obligation to repair the fault. Both the time since the sale and the distance it has traveled are well beyond what would be a "reasonable" warranty for a car of this age and mileage.

 Food for Thought

Legal responsibility is intended to mediate between the seller's and the buyer's interests. Whose interests do you think the legal requirement satisfies best? Is this law a good proxy for biblical law? Why or why not?

_____

_____

_____

_____

_____

_____

_____

_____

Prayer

Pause for a few moments of silence to reflect on this lesson. Then offer a prayer, either spontaneous or by using the following:

> *Lord,*
>
> *I want to represent you well, but I am often tempted to do the bare minimum. Please help me go above and beyond for those I serve.*
>
> *Amen.*

Lesson #2: But What about Moral Principles?

Wayne is satisfied that he is under no legal obligation to pay for the repair, but he is also aware that there may be additional moral responsibility to consider. The law usually defines society's minimum moral requirements for the protection of people.

But Wayne recalls a story he heard from a friend who serves on the board of directors of a company. As the board was discussing a business proposition, their initial conversation agreed the proposition was within the law. Then one of the directors added, "It is legal. But is it right?"

Wayne's friend told him, "As soon as that question was asked, it was followed by a long silence, because we all knew that the answer was no—even before we had time to discuss why."

 *Food for Thought*

Can you think of an instance in your own work where something was allowed but still not right? If so, how was it resolved? How did you feel about the end result?

_____

_____

_____

_____

_____

_____

_____

Wayne knows that the law alone is insufficient guidance. Thinking beyond legal minimum standards, however, is not always easy. What higher standards should a company follow? There was a time in Western society when Christian ethics informed company policy. In the United States, the department store chain J. C. Penney's was famous as "The Golden Rule Store," where it was normal to make a customer service decision based on biblical commands.

But with secularization, religious considerations are no longer an acceptable basis for corporate ethics. And in the absence of biblical ethics, there is now a vacuum of ethical imperative. The only guidance remaining is the legal requirement. The company directors knew the inadequacy of this attitude. Something *was* wrong, but they had no words to talk about it.

Food for Thought

Consider a biblical command you are aware of that might apply
to Wayne's case. What are the difficulties he might experience in
applying it?

_____

_____

_____

_____

_____

_____

Regardless of the limitations of a secular morality, a Christian
approach to ethics looks for some command from God that will
clearly name what is right and wrong. In some cases, it's not hard
to find Bible verses that speak about work and employment issues.
In others, it can be difficult to identify, understand, or apply Bible
verses properly. Next, we will look at how to apply the Bible to
an ethical dilemma.

Prayer

Pause for a few moments of silence to reflect on this lesson. Then
offer a prayer, either spontaneous or by using the following:

Lord,

*I fear living in a society where equity and moral concerns
are lacking. Help me build an awareness of your ethical
principles so that your name and your word are highly
regarded in my workplace.*

Amen.

Lesson #3: A Rule for Every Occasion?

Wayne proceeds to buy *The Businessman's Topical Bible*. He finds that the author, Mike Murdock, lists 1,550 verses from the Bible that claim to "provide God's insight into situations and circumstances encountered every day in today's business world." He simply lists Bible verses he thinks are relevant to each situation, implying that they apply directly and are self-explanatory. Wayne finds some topics that he initially thinks might help with his problem:

> "When a Customer Is Dissatisfied" includes verses such as 2 Timothy 2:24: "And the Lord's servant must not quarrel; instead he must be kind to everyone, able to teach, not resentful," and Luke 6:35: "Love your enemies, do good to them, lend to them without expecting to get anything back. Then your reward will be great."

> "The Businessman and Integrity" includes Psalm 112:5: "Good will come to him who is generous and lends freely, who conducts his affairs with justice."

> "The Businessman and Negotiation" includes 2 Timothy 1:7: "For God did not give us a spirit of timidity, but a spirit of power, of love and of self-discipline."

 Food for Thought

How satisfactorily do these verses function as problem-solvers? Are there any drawbacks to this approach?

_____

_____

_____

_____

_____

_____

Wayne is confused about this collection of Bible verses. Second Timothy 2:24 seems to give advice contrary to 2 Timothy 1:7, which is about teaching, not refunds. Luke 6:35 is about enemies, not customers.

When we start with a "problem" and go looking for an "answer," we approach the Scriptures in a back-to-front way. Making Scripture fit our preformatted schemes ignores consistent themes throughout the Bible that need to be found through deep engagement with the text.

Under the heading "When a Customer Is Dissatisfied," Wayne notices that Luke 21:19 has been taken out of context. "By standing firm you will gain life" has absolutely nothing to do with a dissatisfied customer in business. This also applies to other verses in the sections Wayne looks at.

 Food for Thought

The context for Luke 21:19 involves standing up for Jesus at the end of the age. Does the context of the Scripture affect whether or not it pertains to Wayne's decision? Why or why not?

_____

_____

_____

_____

_____

_____

_____

A danger of hunting out a scriptural rule for every occasion is that we can descend into reductionism and legalism. Witness the scribes and the Pharisees. Their own good intentions blinded them to their arrogant legalism, which opposed their desire to follow God. In seriously trying to apply the Scriptures to the whole of life, they tried to define a rule for every occasion.

This led to an explosion of rules that surpassed the Scriptures yet still failed to cover every situation. They became captive to their own self-constructed rules, and in doing so found themselves obstructing rather than assisting others to fulfill the intention of the law. This is why Jesus says in Matthew 23:13 (ESV),

> "But woe to you, scribes and Pharisees, hypocrites! For you shut the kingdom of heaven in people's faces. For you neither enter yourselves nor allow those who would enter to go in."

Not only does the Bible fail to account for the thousands of situations that arise in business, but in trying to make it do so we risk forcing it to say something it was never intended to mean—or even worse, we trivialize Scripture and miss the point altogether.

Nevertheless, many statements in Scripture are easily applied to simple work issues. If Scripture tells us, as in Colossians 3:22, to work wholeheartedly for our bosses, then we should do this. If it warns us against laziness and not taking responsibility for earning our keep, as in 2 Thessalonians 3:10–12, then we should be energetic about seeking paid employment. These are simple commands and not ethical dilemmas of the sort Wayne is facing.

Food for Thought

How helpful has *The Businessman's Topical Bible* been to Wayne? Do you prefer books that summarize the Bible over the Bible? Why or why not?

_____

_____

_____

_____

_____

_____

_____

_____

Prayer

Pause for a few moments of silence to reflect on this lesson. Then offer a prayer, either spontaneous or by using the following:

Lord,

In my eagerness to apply your word to every aspect of my life, help me to never conform your word to any particular agenda. Grant that I might read your word in its wholeness to appreciate your own purpose.

Amen.

Chapter 4

Case Study—The Broken Gearbox (Continued)

Lesson #1: A Guiding Principle or an Overarching Principle?

Wayne next finds on his bookshelf *Business by the Book: The Complete Guide of Biblical Principles for Business Men and Women*. In this book, author Larry Burkett identifies biblical precepts that are more general than rules, yet are still commands about the right thing to do.

Burkett's book assumes that God has laid down in principles the necessary ethical instructions for "doing business his way." Fundamental to this are the Ten Commandments, which Burkett considers to be the minimum standard separating God's people from those around them. From these and "other minimums that set apart God's followers from others in the business world," Burkett develops "six basic biblical business minimums" (as described on page 12).

While these are not rules found in the Bible, Burkett believes they can be directly deduced from the rules in the Bible. The purpose of his approach is to cover more of the situations that arise in today's workplace by creating principles that are broader than specific rules from Scripture.

 *Food for Thought*

What biblical stories or commands do you see reflected in this list of principles? Is this list broad enough to encompass Wayne's dilemma? Is it specific enough to solve it?

_____

_____

_____

_____

_____

_____

_____

_____

Wayne finds agreement with Burkett's principles about providing "a quality product at a fair price" and treating "your customers fairly." But this doesn't help him know what to do next—a common problem with command-based methods. If the set of commands is specific, then it won't cover the range of situations that occur in the world. If it is general, then it won't provide specific solutions to the problems that do arise.

Wayne remains wary of Burkett's prescriptive approach that seems to reduce Scripture to a "how-to" manual. *Business by the Book* addresses the challenge to let our faith influence the world of business in practical ways, but it is built around a limited set of principles shaped by one author. So while it provides helpful insights into some issues, it also promises more than it can deliver.

Wayne's continued search leads him to John Maxwell's *There's No Such Thing as "Business" Ethics*, and its title appears promising. Maxwell thinks we have made Christian decision-making far too complex. It's his belief that the Bible's moral imperatives can essentially be reduced to just one overarching command. Maxwell suggests there's no such thing as business ethics, only the "Golden Rule" proclaimed by Jesus in the Sermon on the Mount: "So whatever you wish that others would do to you, do also to them, for this is the Law and the Prophets" (Matt. 7:12). Maxwell says that asking "How would I like to be treated in this situation?" should govern all ethical decision-making. He describes this rule as simple, but not easy. Wayne likes this Golden Rule approach to business ethics because it is grounded in the teachings of Jesus rather than evading Jesus and his ethics.

 Food for Thought

Consider an ethical issue you experienced in your workplace, but now apply the Golden Rule to that situation. Explain how it helps or doesn't help you resolve the problem.

_____

_____

_____

_____

_____

_____

_____

Prayer

Pause for a few moments of silence to reflect on this lesson. Then offer a prayer, either spontaneous or by using the following:

> *Lord,*
>
> *Your Golden Rule tells me how to relate to others—as I would have them do to me. But my heart is sometimes miserly or deceitful. Help me to find integrity through the fullness of your word in Scripture.*
>
> *Amen.*

Lesson #2: Does This Help Wayne?

Wayne finds the Golden Rule principle clarifying, because it comes from the heart of Jesus' ethical teaching. He asks, "How would I want to be treated if I were in my customer's shoes?" In doing so, however, Wayne finds he doesn't really understand his customer's perspective. Can the customer truly expect a warranty beyond twelve months after driving 22,000 kilometers (or about 13,600 miles)? Would Wayne expect that for himself if the situation were reversed?

A bigger limitation of the single-maxim approach is the assumption that only two players are affected by the decision. Wayne realizes that his decision to repair the car or not impacts his family and the family of the customer, not to mention his employees who rely on his profitability to maintain their jobs.

Food for Thought

In your work, who is impacted by a decision to suffer a loss for the sake of a client? How does it complicate the decision-making process when many people are involved?

_____

_____

_____

_____

_____

_____

_____

_____

Three Balancing Principles

Perhaps another book can help Wayne with his problem. As we discussed in chapter 1, Alexander Hill, a professor of business and economics, attempts to find a middle way between the simplistic single-rule approach and complicated approaches with multiple rules in his book *Just Business: Christian Ethics for the Marketplace.*

Hill's central point is that Christian ethics in business should be built on the changeless character of God rather than on rules. By study and observation of God's character, we can learn to imitate God: "Behavior consistent with God's character is ethical—that which is not is unethical."

The big question for us in emulating God's character is: "So what is God like?" Hill's answer is that the three characteristics of God most often emphasized in the Bible are holiness, justice, and love.

1. *Holiness.* Pursuing holiness involves the single-minded pursuit of God, which means considering ambitions such as personal relationships, career goals, and material gain as lesser priorities. Pursuing holiness includes zeal, purity, accountability, and humility, as in Colossians 3:2, 5 (ESV): "Set your minds on things that are above, not on things that are on earth. . . . Put to death therefore what is earthly in you: sexual immorality, impurity, passion, evil desire, and covetousness, which is idolatry."

2. *Justice.* Justice is a way of describing the reciprocal rights and duties of people living in community with one another. An example is laid out in Isaiah 1:17 (ESV): "Learn to do good; seek justice, correct oppression, bring justice to the fatherless, plead the widow's cause." God's justice requires that all people be treated with dignity and the opportunity to exercise their free will. These are biblical rights. Rights and duties exist in tension, providing a necessary counterbalance to each other. For example, a worker's right to a livable wage means the employer has a duty to pay the employee fairly. And it also requires the worker to work faithfully for his or her pay. Justice cuts both ways.

3. *Love.* Love is generally viewed as the preeminent virtue, as in Mark 12:29–31 (ESV) when Jesus states the greatest commandment: "The most important is, 'Hear, O Israel: The Lord our God, the Lord is one. And you shall love the Lord your God with all your heart and with all your soul and with all your mind and with all your strength.'

The second is this: 'You shall love your neighbor as your-self.' There is no other commandment greater than these." Love's emphasis is on relationships. Love builds bonds through empathy, mercy, and self-sacrifice. As we shall see in the next section, our practice of love must be moderated by justice and holiness.

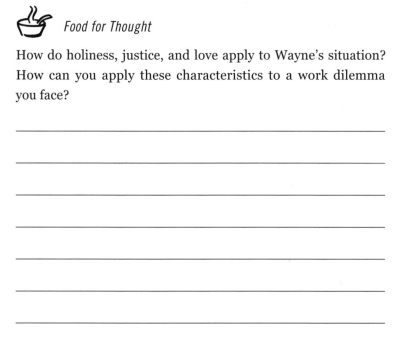 *Food for Thought*

How do holiness, justice, and love apply to Wayne's situation? How can you apply these characteristics to a work dilemma you face?

_____

_____

_____

_____

_____

_____

_____

_____

A Three-Legged Stool

For Hill, "a business act is ethical if it reflects God's holy-just-loving character." There is no significance to the ordering of these characteristics, which are actually intertwined. The image Hill uses for this relatedness is that of a three-legged stool.

If we are to operate biblically in business, then all three "legs" must be taken into account; otherwise the stool is unstable:

1. When holiness is overemphasized to the exclusion of love and justice, the result will be legalism, self-righteous judgmentalism, and withdrawal from society.

2. When justice dominates, then harshness, emotional coldness, and condemnation are the likely outcomes.

3. When love is the only major measure, permissiveness and favoritism arise, because there are no other moral compass points to direct us to the boundaries that love requires.

Wayne appreciates that the author of *Just Business* condemns attempts to reduce Scripture to a book of rules for specific business situations, even as he is acutely aware of the complexities of the business world.

Prayer

Pause for a few moments of silence to reflect on this lesson. Then offer a prayer, either spontaneous or by using the following:

Lord,

Let me learn from your character to know your holiness, your justice, and your love. Help me to be single-minded in my love for you, fair toward others, and always concerned for peace in my relationships.

Amen.

Lesson #3: How Is Wayne Helped by Hill's Approach?

Although Wayne remains unsure about practical holiness in his situation, he finds the balancing principles of justice and love quite useful. What rights and duties exist in his seller-customer relationship? And what response to the customer's request might be just for both parties? Wayne considers that he may have a duty to contribute to the repair, but he thinks the customer also has a responsibility to contribute.

Wayne sold the Camry with a small profit margin, so he feels that expecting him to pay for the entire repair would be unfair. But the principle of love causes him to ask, "What might it mean for me to love this person?" While he sees no clear answer, the question prompts Wayne to consider the customer's financial situation. What impact will a large repair bill have on his customer?

One of the great strengths of the three-legged stool approach is that it provides clarity when considering complex ethical dilemmas without being simplistic.

The main limitation of the three-legged stool is that we're still left with the challenge of determining exactly what is holy, just, and loving for the affected parties. And what do we do when what is just conflicts with our sense of love? How are holiness, justice, and love intertwined in God? Can we really say which gets priority in a given situation? The danger Wayne begins to see is that he might cease looking to the character of Jesus and instead turn holiness, justice, and love into abstract ideas. The stool image indeed has its limits.

 *Food for Thought*

Consider Deuteronomy 10:18 (ESV): "He executes justice for the fatherless and the widow, and loves the sojourner, giving him food and clothing." What do you make of the interplay between God's justice and love in this passage? What difference does it make that these are God's character attributes, not just ethical ideas?

_____

_____

_____

_____

_____

_____

_____

Wayne is beginning to feel he's making progress. It was always obvious that reaching a decision would not be easy, but his search has given him a hunger to know Jesus better in order to apply to his situation a better sense of holiness, justice, and love.

Whatever approach to ethics we adopt, discerning and balancing the relevant rules and principles we discover in Scripture is an important part. Wayne sees that specific biblical commands must be read in their context and in the overarching purpose of the Bible. He sees that while it is important to remember the Golden Rule, it has real limits in our urbanizing world where many people are affected by business decisions.

An approach guiding him to look more deeply into the character of God as revealed in Jesus also encourages Wayne in his quest for better business ethics as a Christian. But his last reading gives him the further prompt to also try to calculate the consequences of different courses of action to see which decisions produce the most loving, just, and holy results.

Prayer

Pause for a few moments of silence to reflect on this lesson. Then offer a prayer, either spontaneous or by using the following:

Lord,

I would rather see holiness, justice, and love as abstractions than as character traits I need to build in myself. Help me transform my mind to be more like yours. You are wonderful, God.

Amen.

Chapter 5

Consequences

Lesson #1: The Most Moral Course of Action

Until now, Wayne has asked, "What rules should I follow?" So he looked for rules or principles from the Bible. But since biblical rules did not provide Wayne with a clear answer, he's ready to try a different approach. Wayne now wonders if he can figure out which potential solution to the broken gearbox problem will produce the best result. He reasons that if he examines the potential consequences of each response and compares the likely results, then he might be able to make a decision based on the best outcome.

The ethical technique of comparing potential consequences is often known as "consequentialism" or "teleological" ethics—from the Greek word *telos* meaning "end." Unlike the command approach (where the best option is determined by whether the action conforms to an applicable rule), the consequences approach is entirely focused on the outcome. To borrow a popular aphorism, the end justifies the means.

 Food for Thought

Was there a time at your job that you made a decision based on potential consequences? What were the benefits of such an approach? Can you think of any drawbacks?

_____

_____

_____

_____

_____

_____

_____

_____

The Bible and Consequences

In the Bible, as in life, some decisions lead to greater blessing while others lead to terrible consequences. Ezekiel 18 highlights the different sorts of actions that bring blessings or curses:

> If a man is righteous and does what is lawful and right—if he does not eat upon the mountains or lift up his eyes to the idols of the house of Israel, does not defile his neighbor's wife or approach a woman during her menstrual period, does not oppress anyone, but restores to the debtor his pledge, commits no robbery, gives his bread to the hungry and covers the naked with a garment, does not take advance or accrued interest, withholds his hand from iniquity, executes true justice between contending parties, follows my statutes, and is careful to observe my ordinances, acting faithfully—such a one is righteous; he shall surely live, says the Lord God.
>
> If he has a son who is violent, a shedder of blood, who does any of these things (though his father does none of them), who eats upon the mountains, defiles his neighbor's wife, oppresses the poor and needy, commits robbery, does not restore the pledge, lifts up his eyes to the idols, commits abomination, takes advance or accrued interest; shall he then live? He shall not. He has done all these abominable things; he shall surely die; his blood shall be upon himself. (Ezek. 18:5-13)

According to Ezekiel, our actions have consequences that directly affect our lives. We certainly see this with practices that are self-evidently good or evil, like the ones Ezekiel lists above. But even small decisions, like whether or not to extend forgiveness, carry spiritual consequences. Jesus warns his listeners: "If you do not forgive others, neither will your Father forgive your trespasses" (Matt. 6:15).

 Food for Thought

Sometimes a consequences approach to ethics calls us to search for "the greater good." What is "the good" implied in Jesus' teaching above?

_____

_____

_____

_____

_____

_____

_____

_____

Measuring the Good

Should Wayne repair the customer's car at his own expense, or should he tell the customer no? As he thinks about the potential consequences of each decision, four awkward questions arise:

1. What is good? How do we define "good"? Presumably it is more than simply making the customer—or Wayne—financially better off.

2. Good for whom? Who really benefits from this decision? Is it only Wayne and his customer who are involved? What about Wayne's employees or potential future customers?

3. Can the good be calculated? Can we know with 100 percent accuracy what will be the result of each action?

4. Good in what context? Can things that are good in one context be bad in another?

 Food for Thought

Apply these four questions to an ethical dilemma you face in your work. Do they help you compare potential results? Or do they make the comparison less clear?

_____

_____

_____

_____

_____

_____

_____

Prayer

Pause for a few moments of silence to reflect on this lesson. Then offer a prayer, either spontaneous or by using the following:

> *Lord,*
>
> *I see that the more I think about ethics, the more thoughtfulness I need. Help me to deepen my understanding so that I may fully represent you in my workplace.*
>
> *Amen.*

Lesson #2: What Is Good?

Wanting to delve deeper into the question of "What is good?" Wayne discovers the most popular form of consequentialist thinking: utilitarianism. Utilitarianism defines "good" as whatever produces the greatest amount of happiness for the greatest number of people. "Happiness" is its primary goal, which implies that pain should in all circumstances be minimized or avoided.

The Bible, however, does not share this opinion of happiness. Jesus turns our thinking about happiness upside down in his Beatitudes when he says:

> "Blessed are you when others revile you and persecute you and utter all kinds of evil against you falsely on my account. Rejoice and be glad, for your reward is great in heaven, for so they persecuted the prophets who were before you." (Matt. 5:11-12 ESV)

Jesus does not call us to maximize our own happiness. Rather, he indicates that suffering, if it's for God's sake, can be a source of joy. It seems that pure utilitarianism is not a perfect match with the gospel.

 *Food for Thought*

Jesus' Beatitudes seem to indicate that real joy in life comes through following him, a path that might include loss and suffering. Is there a tension between this definition of happiness and your own? How do you resolve that tension?

_____

_____

_____

_____

_____

_____

_____

_____

If a secular definition of happiness is not what's considered "good" in the Bible, then what is? The state of the world prior to the Fall is declared "good" and "very good" by God. "And God saw everything that he had made, and behold, it was very good" (Gen. 1:31). This state will be restored and extended when Christ returns again and ushers in the new heaven and the new earth:

> And I heard a loud voice from the throne saying, "Behold, the dwelling place of God is with man. He will dwell with them, and they will be his people, and God himself will be with them as their God. He will wipe away every tear from their eyes, and death shall be no more, neither shall there be mourning, nor crying, nor pain anymore, for the former things have passed away."
>
> (Rev. 21:3–4 ESV)

The history of Israel, the life, death, and resurrection of Jesus, and God's provision for the Christian community all have as their primary purpose the restoration of life lived in intimacy with God. With God, happiness is the by-product of his primary intention, which is to make us whole as we were originally created to be.

The New Testament is clear that embracing suffering and pain is often the road to wholeness—whether for us or those whom our suffering helps. We can take as our model the choice Jesus made to submit to the cross: "The Son of Man came not to be served but to serve, and to give his life a ransom for many" (Matt. 20:28).

 Food for Thought

How would you define goodness in Wayne's case? What course of action do you think would fulfill God's purpose of redemption?

Prayer

Pause for a few moments of silence to reflect on this lesson. Then offer a prayer, either spontaneous or by using the following:

Lord,

As we consider what is good, help us to remember and trust that you have an eternal good in mind for your people. Help us work toward your good ends, to the benefit of all around us.

Amen.

Lesson #3: The Greater Good

A more popular form of consequentialist thinking advocates that "the greater good" should be the yardstick for our ethical decisions. People who use this approach say that the best decision is the one that will bring about the greatest good for the greatest number of people. We have discussed utilitarianism, which seeks to maximize happiness for the greatest number. This means that a course of action is not good if it only makes a few people happy but makes things worse for a large number of people. Conversely, an act can be good if it makes many people happy at the expense of a few.

But what if making decisions based on the good of the majority has potentially negative or disastrous consequences for the minority— particularly if that minority is a marginalized and largely powerless group? Under such ends-justifies-the-means terms, all manner of evil has been condoned throughout world history.

The Bible consistently calls God's people to stand up for and protect the poor and the marginalized. The Old Testament prophets regularly challenged the people of God to care for the most vulnerable, even declaring that the health of a society is measured by how they treat the "orphan, widow, and alien" (three significant marginalized groups).

> "You shall not pervert the justice due to your poor in his lawsuit.
> . . . You shall not oppress a sojourner. You know the heart of a
> sojourner, for you were sojourners in the land of Egypt."
> (Exod. 23:6, 9 ESV)

> "Then I will draw near to you for judgment. I will be a swift witness
> against the sorcerers, against the adulterers, against those who
> swear falsely, against those who oppress the hired worker in his
> wages, the widow and the fatherless, against those who thrust
> aside the sojourner, and do not fear me, says the Lord of hosts."
> (Mal. 3:5 ESV)

 Food for Thought

What is the ethical message in God's concern for these three groups of marginalized people? What does this mean for the application of the "greater good" yardstick?

_____

_____

_____

_____

_____

_____

_____

_____

The Meaning for Wayne

As Wayne sees it, there are really only two parties who might be affected by his decision—himself and the customer. Many other decisions he faces as a car dealer involve indefinable consequences relating to their impact on environmental, social, and community issues. But this choice is rather simpler.

What good will result from a decision to pay for or at least contribute to the repair? The answer is that he will have a satisfied customer, saving him from unnecessary financial hardship. This may serve the greater good better than not paying for the repair and benefiting personally in the short term.

Frequently, we have no real way of knowing what consequences will result from our actions, or indeed how to rate or measure the good. For this reason, both commands and consequences should be taken into account.

Commands often serve to guide us toward actions that can reasonably be expected to lead to good outcomes. For example, the command "Do not lie" is very likely to lead to better consequences than its opposite, especially in complex situations in which it would be hard to predict the consequences of telling even a well-intentioned "white" lie. At the same time, paying attention to the consequences often helps us determine which rules apply in which circumstances. "Do not murder" applies in all circumstances because the consequence is death, which cannot be undone by human power.

But "Honor the Sabbath day" does not apply in the sense of preventing you from healing a person who is sick on the Sabbath, because the consequence of pain and suffering is antithetical to God's restoration of the world to the state he intends for it. See this example:

Now he was teaching in one of the synagogues on the Sabbath. And behold, there was a woman who had had a disabling spirit for eighteen years. She was bent over and could not fully straighten herself. When Jesus saw her, he called her over and said to her, "Woman, you are freed from your disability." And he laid his hands on her, and immediately she was made straight, and she glorified God. But the ruler of the synagogue, indignant because Jesus had healed on the Sabbath, said to the people, "There are six days in which work ought to be done. Come on those days and be healed, and not on the Sabbath day." Then the Lord answered him, "You hypocrites! Does not each of you on the Sabbath untie his ox or his donkey from the manger and lead it away to water it? And ought not this woman, a daughter of Abraham whom Satan bound for eighteen years, be loosed from this bond on the Sabbath day?"

(Luke 13:10–16 ESV)

Prayer

Pause for a few moments of silence to reflect on this lesson. Then offer a prayer, either spontaneous or by using the following:

Lord,

It is humbling when we realize that even our well-intentioned ethical decisions can have unforeseen consequences that harm others. Please help us develop the humility and the sensitivity to test our decisions carefully when the good of many others is at stake.

Amen

Chapter 6

Consequences and Character

Lesson #1: Good in What Context?

Context—having regard for the situation in which something happens—is important in ethical decision-making. When actions mean different things among people of different cultures, an ethical response in one culture will be different in another.

Many times, the apostle Paul was faced with dilemmas of context. In 1 Corinthians 8, for instance, he examined ethical decisions that arise from eating food offered to idols:

> Therefore, as to the eating of food offered to idols, we know that "an idol has no real existence," and that "there is no God but one." . . . However, not all possess this knowledge. But some, through former association with idols, eat food as really offered to an idol, and their conscience, being weak, is defiled. Food will not commend us to God. We are no worse off if we do not eat, and no better off if we do. But take care that this right of yours does not somehow become a stumbling block to the weak. For if anyone sees you who have knowledge eating in an idol's temple, will he not be encouraged, if his conscience is weak, to eat food offered to idols? And so by your knowledge this weak person is destroyed, the brother for whom Christ died. Thus, sinning against your brothers and wounding their conscience when it is weak, you sin against Christ. Therefore, if food makes my brother stumble, I will never eat meat, lest I make my brother stumble.
>
> (1 Cor. 8:4, 7–13 ESV)

The issue Paul raises is how our behavior will affect "weak believers." In this case, Paul put love and consideration for others ahead of his own liberty to do as he saw fit. The question was not just "Is it right?" but rather "What outcomes will it lead to?" What he felt free to do in one situation, he chose not to do in another where it might cause offense. Paul decided on the rightness or wisdom of the action according to the consequences in its context.

 Food for Thought

Two teenagers in a residential employment training camp broke the rules, snuck out at night, and were caught shoplifting. The leader of the pair, from a wealthy family in a neighboring country, was expelled from the project; the other, the son of an immigrant whose mother had been abandoned, was retained in the project and graduated. What is your opinion of the decision-making by the project leader? What are the circumstances that help you decide if it was ethical or not?

An ethical response to context is not the same as moral relativism. For example, the command not to lie is an absolute standard. Yet it applies differently in different contexts. "Did you pay for this already?" requires a "yes" or a "no," whereas "Does this shirt look good on me?" might require "Sort of" or "It's not bad, but there might be better ones."

Our societies are increasingly multicultural, and so we must expect to face situations where the context challenges us to change our practices. As an employer, how do you allocate bereavement leave when several of your staff members are from ethnic backgrounds where it is culturally essential for them to take several days, a number of times a year, to attend the funerals of relatives and friends?

It's not just cross-cultural situations that require us to adapt. It's also a factor in working out whether we treat people differently because of their circumstances. For example, a doctor might use graduated fees for patients based on their income. A car dealer might take a person's economic circumstances into account when negotiating a price, as Flow Automotive did when they realized that poor people tend to end up paying more for cars because they're often less practiced in negotiations.

Wayne starts thinking about ways that his particular context might influence possible courses of action. He already noted his concern for the customer's financial situation. Wayne needs to know the likely financial impact the cost of the repair will bring on the customer and the customer's family. Is it likely to cause undue hardship? Wayne thinks this is worth taking into consideration. In fact, for him it is part of the wider question of love and justice.

Wayne wonders if the customer is generous and liberal with his own time and money—serving others and genuinely seeking to make a difference in the world. If this is the case, he may feel it is extra fitting to extend generosity toward the man. At the same time, Wayne also needs to consider what he can afford and the implications for him and his own family if he loses money on this transaction.

But then another angle comes to his mind: Should Wayne think carefully about the sort of precedent he is setting? If he takes a soft line, will other customers also come running for assistance? Wayne shrugs at the possibility. For him, personally, this is not a major issue. The other factors he has sifted through, as far as he is concerned, are of much greater importance. He doesn't mind if he acquires a reputation as a "soft touch," as long as he is satisfied with the appropriateness of his choice.

Wayne now realizes how personal ethics can become, and he has to think about how his own character is being shaped as he makes his choices.

 Food for Thought

How does reputation fit into your decision-making? Are you concerned about being seen as hard or soft by those you work with? Why or why not?

_____

_____

_____

_____

_____

_____

_____

Prayer

Pause for a few moments of silence to reflect on this lesson. Then offer a prayer, either spontaneous or by using the following:

Lord,

The world is complex, and so are the people in it. And yet you love them all. Help me to understand the people I work with, in all the complexities of their circumstances, so that I may love them as you do.

Amen.

Lesson #2: The Character Approach

So far, Wayne has calculated his decision-making through an analysis of commands and consequences, which focus on the morality of the action or choice to be made. But issues of character focus on the person making the decision. As we have seen, this is often called "virtue" or "character" ethics, because its chief concern is the character of the person performing the action.

Instead of asking "What is right?" or "What will produce the best results?" character ethics asks, "What type of person should I become?" The assumption is that if we truly yearn to reflect God's character, then this will increasingly lead to doing the right thing. Character ethics also recognizes our human nature—knowing the right thing to do doesn't ensure we will do it! It takes character to do the right thing, and this is because doing the right thing is often costly.

When we considered the essentials of God's character earlier—love, justice, and holiness—our aim was to use those characteristics as a straightedge by which to align our decision-making. This is a command approach because it is about following God's character as a command, not necessarily being shaped by it. In the character approach, we ask how our actions will form our characters. This requires a subtle change of emphasis. We must look at how God's character shapes our own characters. As Christians, we want the holiness, justice, and love of God ingrained in us as a default setting.

The following verses focus on the growth of character:

> Do not be conformed to this world, but be transformed by the renewal of your mind, that by testing you may discern what is the will of God, what is good and acceptable and perfect.
>
> (Rom. 12:2 ESV)

> Therefore, preparing your minds for action, and being sober-minded, set your hope fully on the grace that will be brought to you at the revelation of Jesus Christ. As obedient children, do not be conformed to the passions of your former ignorance, but as he who called you is holy, you also be holy in all your conduct, since it is written, "You shall be holy, for I am holy."
>
> (1 Pet. 1:13–16 ESV)

 Food for Thought

According to the passages above, what is the means by which we become shaped in the character of Christ?

_____

_____

_____

_____

_____

Thus far we have discussed an idealized decision-making process, where we have time and ability to analyze complex issues. Sometimes the process is like this, but other times we have to make decisions on the run. How we respond to a complaint from our boss or sort out a misunderstanding with a customer—these decisions often occur instinctively. We can expect our decisions to be far more reliable if we have the habit of working on godly character. Iris Murdoch has said, "At crucial moments of choice, most of the business of choosing is already over." Or as Scripture would put it:

> For this very reason, make every effort to supplement your faith with virtue, and virtue with knowledge, and knowledge with self-control, and self-control with steadfastness, and steadfastness with godliness, and godliness with brotherly affection, and brotherly affection with love. For if these qualities are yours and are increasing, they keep you from being ineffective or unfruitful in the knowledge of our Lord Jesus Christ. (2 Pet. 1:5–8 ESV)

 Food for Thought

What are the issues Peter lays out for character development? How does he suggest we develop these traits in our lives?

_____

_____

_____

_____

_____

_____

Prayer

Pause for a few moments of silence to reflect on this lesson. Then offer a prayer, either spontaneous or by using the following:

Lord,

I accept that my character is shaped by the desires to which I give expression. Please help me to repent of the longings that lead me away from you, and grant me a purity of heart that desires to follow you and you only.

Amen.

Lesson #3: How Can Character Change Wayne's Decision?

Wayne is now aware that rather than finding it easy to resist the customer's complaint about the car and his request to fix it, his heart has gone out to the customer. Wayne genuinely wants to respond in a way that expresses care and concern. Reflecting on the slow but real development of Christian character throughout his lifetime, he now recognizes (and values) compassion, kindness, and generosity.

So he finds himself wanting to respond positively to the customer's request. As he calculates the consequences, he begins to think more about how far he can go in providing assistance rather than how much he can resist the customer's request. It seems that Wayne's default setting has already been shaped by Jesus' values.

 *Food for Thought*

Do you recognize the default settings that govern your automatic responses to others? What do these tell you about your own character?

_____

_____

_____

_____

_____

_____

_____

_____

We are to become like Jesus, whose character and virtues we understand through the narrative story of the Gospels. Despite our intentions, however, we absorb the gospel narrative through the filter of our cultures. The way we retell this story—what virtues we emphasize, what failures we highlight, and how we encourage one another to nurture the habits and practices it describes—all of these have a significant impact on how we grow in virtue.

We must acknowledge that all faith communities will tend to reframe Jesus in ways that are less challenging to their own lifestyle and worldview. For Western churches of wealth and affluence, the danger is to unconsciously filter out the enormous socioeconomic, political, and environmental implications of Jesus' life and teachings. This results in a Jesus who limits himself to issues of sexual conduct and personal honesty. However important those might be, this is not the full picture of Jesus in the Gospels. Jesus models and teaches a consistent ethic for life that encompasses the issues of sex, wealth, and power in our families, social lives, and every day in our work.

 Food for Thought

What are the key character attributes that your faith community promotes? What blind spots do you see in your own retelling of the gospel?

_____

_____

_____

_____

_____

_____

_____

Prayer

Pause for a few moments of silence to reflect on this lesson. Then offer a prayer, either spontaneous or by using the following:

> *Lord,*
>
> *Help me to reflect Jesus' character completely, as revealed in the Gospels. Let my heart be stirred by your word so that I may feel compassion for those around me and make ethical decisions in my work.*
>
> *Amen*

Chapter 7

Developing the Character of Jesus in the Workplace

Lesson #1: Virtue Ethics Has Important Lessons to Teach Us

Throughout this study, we have discovered that making ethical decisions in the marketplace is much more than developing a good decision-making process. It's even more than agreeing to a "Code of Ethics," or considering the consequences of our decisions. It is who we are becoming that will substantially shape our ethical choices.

We cannot develop godly character alone. We need others. When we are committed to a community seeking to retell, understand, embrace, and live out the gospel story, we are much more likely to become people of virtue. And the world of business certainly needs people of character.

Such communities must find ways of discovering a clearer picture of the character of Jesus, of asking the hard and uncomfortable questions that help us confront our limited view of the virtuous life. When this happens, we are less likely to duplicate the many sad examples of Christians doing business in a thoroughly ungodly manner.

Food for Thought

How would you characterize your own Christian journey? How
has your character changed over time? Do you have a community
of other Christians to help you further develop?

_____

_____

_____

_____

_____

_____

Putting It All Together

Commands, consequences, and character are three different approaches to making ethical decisions. In the case study of Wayne
and his customer's gearbox problem, Wayne arrived at a moment of self-discovery that went beyond rules or consequences—
although these were involved in his processing. Wayne was part
of a Christian community that drew from the gospel story great
value for the kindness, compassion, and generosity of Jesus. This
influenced his default setting, so that Wayne was not defensive
when he heard about his customer's request; rather, he was will-
ing to consider what the repair meant for his customer and be
empathetic to that person's pain.

What was Wayne's final decision? He chose to assist the customer
by sharing the cost of the repair equally.

In our own everyday dilemmas, most of us will process ethical questions through a combination of approaches. That's because it's hard to apply specific commands or rules without also considering the consequences of such actions. At the same time, when we weigh and compare different consequences, we need to identify the rules that will lead to those results. In the end, regardless of whatever we've decided in theory, it is actually character and openness to the nudging of God's Holy Spirit that dictate how we act.

Consider this example from Jesus' life:

> Then Jesus was led up by the Spirit into the wilderness to be tempted by the devil. And after fasting forty days and forty nights, he was hungry. And the tempter came and said to him, "If you are the Son of God, command these stones to become loaves of bread." But he answered, "It is written, 'Man shall not live by bread alone, but by every word that comes from the mouth of God.'"
>
> (Matt. 4:1–4 ESV)

 Food for Thought

How does Jesus react to his moment of temptation? What character traits does this display? What factors do you imagine influenced Jesus' character up to this point?

_____

_____

_____

_____

_____

_____

Prayer

Pause for a few moments of silence to reflect on this lesson. Then offer a prayer, either spontaneous or by using the following:

> *Lord,*
>
> *Thank you for the positive forces that shape my character. Please help me to overcome pride and a tendency toward independence as I make decisions that have consequences for others.*
>
> *Amen.*

Lesson #2: Summary of the Three Approaches

Our study on ethics can be summarized in the following Decision Model for Major Moral Dilemmas:

Determine the right thing to do in each situation.

1. Define the applicable rules (commands)

2. Discern the best outcomes (consequences)

3. Become a virtuous person by doing the right thing in situation after situation

4. Do what you have determined is right (character)

The recommended method usually involves doing the following:

- Gather all the relevant facts

- Clarify the key ethical issues

- Identify rules and principles relevant for the case

- Consult the important sources of guidance—especially the Bible—with sensitivity to the best way of reading the Bible to address this situation

- Ask for help from others in your community who know you and the situation; this will help you avoid self-deception and paying too much attention to your particular biases

- List all the alternative courses of action

- Compare the alternatives with the principles involved

- Calculate the likely results of each course of action and consider the consequences

- Consider your decision prayerfully before God

- Make your decision and act on it

- Find ways to continuously practice the activities inherent in doing what is right, as you have determined

 Food for Thought

What type of situation do you think would require this exhaustive methodology for determining the best response? Do you face such weighty decisions in your line of work? Is the framework above helpful for you?

_____

_____

_____

_____

_____

_____

Prayer

Pause for a few moments of silence to reflect on this lesson. Then offer a prayer, either spontaneous or by using the following:

> *Lord,*
>
> *In the past I have treated ethical decisions more thoughtlessly than I should have. Help me to realize how my decisions will impact the lives of others, not only immediately but also in the long term. Grant me the courage to do what is truly ethical in your view.*
>
> *Amen.*

Lesson #3: Everyday Moral Choices

Most ethical decisions in our daily work are made instantly, often under pressure and without much room for forethought. They are almost instinctive—the product of lifelong habits, shaped by the culture of the places in which we work and by the peer groups and faith communities to which we belong.

Such decisions are influenced by the extent to which Christian virtues and character have been molded into the core of our beings. It is easy to overlook the limitation of our understanding of Jesus' character, as it is often a blind spot in the communities that helped shape us.

The importance of *being* as the foundation for our *doing* doesn't mean we don't need moral reasoning. Within the virtuous life, there is still a place for understanding rules and calculating consequences, but here the rules and consequences are subordinated to the virtues. We can view them as servants rather than as masters.

For example, even a person with the virtue of honesty has to understand and obey the rules of Generally Accepted Accounting Principles (or, outside the United States, International Financial Reporting Standards) in order to produce accurate financial statements. Terms such as "in our opinion" and "unforeseeable" have particular definitions that must be followed.

But an honest person always uses the rules to increase the overall accuracy of the financial statement, never to find a way to obscure the truth without breaking any laws.

 Food for Thought

Consider the rules that govern your work practices. In what way do they ensure a right outcome for your work? In what way do you see them used for wrong outcomes?

_____

_____

_____

_____

_____

_____

_____

_____

Emphasizing virtue does not eliminate moral dilemmas. In many situations we find ourselves dealing with competing virtues rather than clear-cut good or bad choices. Consider the dilemma you might face when catching a colleague stealing from your workplace. Justice requires punishment, but the circumstances might pull you toward mercy and compassion. Whistle-blowers will often be caught between courage and prudence, and they may take years before choosing courage in order to expose corruption.

Making good moral decisions in these cases is less about seeing one right answer (because there probably is not just one) and more about striving for a balanced Christian response that recognizes all the competing priorities. We must also admit that we live in a fallen world where often there is no one perfect Christian response. Sometimes all courses of action include negative consequences.

Hebrews 5:14 (ESV) exhorts us to new levels of thoughtfulness in our Christian lives: "But solid food is for the mature, for those who have their powers of discernment trained by constant practice to distinguish good from evil."

The grace of God, who has forgiven us to live in freedom, means we no longer have to earn God's approval through slavery to rules and regulations. Nor do we need to perform intellectual gymnastics as we consider all possible outcomes for our actions. Rather, our lives can be shaped by the character of Jesus, who has already set before us good work to do.

> For we are his workmanship, created in Christ Jesus for good works, which God prepared beforehand, that we should walk in them. (Eph. 2:10)

Food for Thought

How would you define Christian ethics now? What has changed in your understanding since you started this study?

_____

_____

_____

_____

_____

_____

_____

_____

Prayer

Pause for a few moments of silence to reflect on this lesson. Then offer a prayer, either spontaneous or by using the following:

Lord,

Thank you for saving me from futility and giving me purposeful work to do. I ask that you would work into my being your will to do what is best, for my sake and for the sake of others. Help me to practice what my heart knows is the best response until it is the habit of my life.

Amen.

Wisdom for Using This Study in the Workplace

Community within the workplace is a good thing and a Christian community within the workplace is even better. Sensitivity is needed, however, when we get together in the workplace (even a Christian workplace) to enjoy fellowship time together, learn what the Bible has to say about our work, and encourage one another in Jesus' name. When you meet at your place of employment, here are some guidelines to keep in mind:

- *Be sensitive to your surroundings.* Know your company policy about having such a group on company property. Make sure not to give the impression that this is a secret or exclusive group.

- *Be sensitive to time constraints.* Don't go over your allotted time. Don't be late to work! Make sure you are a good witness to the others (especially non-Christians) in your workplace by being fully committed to your work during working hours and doing all your work with excellence.

- *Be sensitive to the shy or silent members of your group.* Encourage everyone in the group and give them a chance to talk.

- *Be sensitive to the others by being prepared.* Read the Bible study material and Scripture passages and think about your answers to the questions ahead of time.

These Bible studies are based on the Theology of Work biblical commentary. Besides reading the commentary, please visit the Theology of Work website (www.theologyofwork.org) for videos, interviews, and other material on the Bible and your work.

Leader's Guide

Living Word. It is always exciting to start a new group and study. The possibilities of growth and relationship are limitless when we engage with one another and with God's word. Always remember that God's word is "alive and active, sharper than any double-edged sword" (Heb. 4:12) and when you study his word, it should change you.

A Way Has Been Made. Please know you and each person joining your study have been prayed for by people you will probably never meet who share your faith. And remember that "the LORD himself goes before you and will be with you; he will never leave you nor forsake you. Do not be afraid; do not be discouraged" (Deut. 31:8). As a leader, you need to know that truth. Remind yourself of it throughout this study.

Pray. It is always a good idea to pray for your study and those involved weeks before you even begin. It is recommended to pray for yourself as leader, your group members, and the time you are about to spend together. It's no small thing you are about to start and the more you prepare in the Spirit, the better. Apart from Jesus, we can do nothing (John 14:5). Remain in him and "you will bear much fruit" (John 15:5). It's also a good idea to have trusted friends pray and intercede for you and your group as you work through the study.

Spiritual Battle. Like it or not, the Bible teaches that we are in the middle of a spiritual battle. The enemy would like nothing more than for this study to be ineffective. It would be part of his scheme to have group members not show up or engage in any discussion. His victory would be that your group just passes time together going through the motions of a yet another Bible study. You, as a leader, are a threat to the enemy, as it is your desire to lead people down the path of righteousness (as taught in Proverbs). Read Ephesians 6:10–20 and put your armor on.

Scripture. Prepare before your study by reading the selected Scripture verses ahead of time.

Chapters. Each chapter contains approximately three lessons. As you work through the lessons, keep in mind the particular chapter theme in connection with the lessons. These lessons are designed so that you can go through them in thirty minutes each.

Lessons. Each lesson has teaching points with their own discussion questions. This format should keep the participants engaged with the text and one another.

Food for Thought. The questions at the end of the teaching points are there to create discussion and deepen the connection between each person and the content being addressed. You know the people in your group and should feel free to come up with your own questions or adapt the ones provided to best meet the needs of your group. Again, this would require some preparation beforehand.

Opening and Closing Prayers. Sometimes prayer prompts are given before and usually after each lesson. These are just suggestions. You know your group and the needs present, so please feel free to pray accordingly.

Bible Commentary. The Theology of Work series contains a variety of books to help you apply the Scriptures and Christian faith to your work. This Bible study is based on the *Theology of Work Bible Commentary*, examining what the Bible says about work. This commentary is intended to assist those with theological training or interest to conduct in-depth research into passages or books of Scripture.

Video Clips. The Theology of Work website (www.theologyofwork .org) provides good video footage of people from the marketplace highlighting the teaching from all the books of the Bible. It would be great to incorporate some of these videos into your teaching time.

Enjoy your study! Remember that God's word does not return void—ever. It produces fruit and succeeds in whatever way God has intended it to succeed.

> "So shall my word be that goes out from my mouth;
>   it shall not return to me empty,
> but it shall accomplish that which I purpose,
>   and succeed in the thing for which I sent it." (Isa. 55:11)

"This commentary was written exactly for those of us who aim to integrate our faith and work on a daily basis and is an excellent reminder that God hasn't called the world to go to the church, but has called the Church to go to the world."

BONNIE WURZBACHER

FORMER SENIOR VICE PRESIDENT, THE COCA-COLA COMPANY

Explore what the Bible has to say about work, book by book.

THE BIBLE AND YOUR WORK
Study Series

THEOLOGY OF WORK   PROJECT